P9-BZQ-712

Printed in Hong Kong.

Project editor: Jill Brubaker
Cover and book design: Diane Goldsmith
Cover photograph © B. "Moose" Peterson

Library of Congress Cataloging-in-Publication Data
Wildlife California.
p. cm.—(Chronicle junior nature series)
Summary: Nature guide focusing on the mammals, reptiles, and birds that are found in the wilderness areas of California.
ISBN 0-87701-886-3
1. Zoology—California—Juvenile literature. [1. Zoology—California. 2. Animals.] I. Series
QL164.W56 1991
596.09794—dc20 90-49847
CIP
AC

Distributed in Canada by Raincoast Books, 112 East Third Avenue,
Vancouver, B.C. V5T 1C8

10 9 8 7 6 5 4 3 2 1

Chronicle Books, 275 Fifth Street, San Francisco, California 94103

Acknowledgments

Chronicle Books would like to give special thanks to the following people from California's National Parks for their ideas, suggestions, enthusiasm, and willingness to approve the text and contents of this book: Allen M. Fish, Program Director, Golden Gate National Recreation Area; Norma Craig, Visual Specialist, Yosemite National Park; Len McKenzie, Chief Park Interpreter, Yosemite National Park; Bob Moon, Division Resource Management, Joshua Tree National Monument; Mark Holden, Division Resource Management, Joshua Tree National Monument; Frank Balthis, Ranger, Año Nuevo State Reserve; Ross Hopkins, Chief Naturalist, Death Valley National Monument; Greg Gigichinos, Chief Naturalist, Whiskeytown National Recreation Area; The Redwood Natural History Association, Redwood National Park; Scott Isaakson, Assistant Ranger, Lassen Volcanic National Park.

And to the talented photographers who have contributed to this book:
Frank Balthis ©, p. 32.
Richard Bucich ©, pp. 19, 35, 36.
James W. Cornett ©, pp. 23, 24, 27, 28.
Michael Frye ©, pp. 20, 55.
Howard Hall ©, p. 31.
John Hendrickson ©, pp. 12, 16, 39, 40, 43, 47, 48, 51, 52.
B. "Moose" Peterson/Wildlife Research Photography ©, pp. 8, 11, 44.
Art Wolfe ©, pp. 4, 7, 15.

WILDLIFE
CALIFORNIA

CHRONICLE JUNIOR NATURE SERIES

CHRONICLE BOOKS • SAN FRANCISCO

INTRODUCTION

Judd A. Howell
Wildlife Ecologist
National Park Service

Welcome to the first in an exciting series of photographic guides written especially for young people. When we are outdoors or on a trip, we see animals, sometimes just a glimpse, sometimes longer. Often we wish to know their name. Or we want to know more about them. Where do they live? What do they eat? This book will help you get started. By being your first, but we hope not your last, field guide, you can use this book to begin to know the animals around you.

California has many species of wildlife. Some can be found all across the state, others can be found in only special places. These places where animals live are called habitats. California has a broad diversity of habitats—like mountain forests, coastal grassland, or desert scrub—that provide food and shelter for this remarkable collection of animals.

Some of California's animals, like the red-tailed hawk, are thriving. Other animals, like the kit fox, are not. Animals that aren't doing well are called threatened or endangered. Animals become endangered for many reasons such as people shooting them, polluting their food, or building homes that destroy their habitat.

One way to protect animals is to set aside special wildlife preserves, like our national parks. The national parks are excellent places to see the diversity of California's wildlife. When you visit a park, remember to leave it exactly as you found it. Together, by respecting and understanding the natural world around us, we can learn to protect and preserve our fragile wildlife heritage for ourselves and for future generations. We hope this guide will be a first step toward a lifelong appreciation of the wonders of the wild.

CONTENTS

PAGE	ANIMAL	TYPE OF PARK		
5	Black Bear	●	●	
6	Mule Deer	●	●	●
9	Coyote	●	●	●
10	Kit Fox			●
13	Raccoon	●	●	
14	Porcupine	●	●	●
17	Striped Skunk	●	●	●
18	California Ground Squirrel	●	●	●
21	Lodgepole Chipmunk	●	●	●
22	Desert Cottontail			●
25	Desert Tortoise			●
26	Sidewinder			●
29	Side-blotched Lizard			●
30	Gray Whale	●		
33	Northern Elephant Seal	●		
34	California Sea Lion	●		
37	Sea Otter	●		
38	Golden Eagle	●	●	●
41	Red-tailed Hawk	●	●	●
42	Great Horned Owl	●	●	●
45	Common Raven	●	●	●
46	Roadrunner		●	●
49	Acorn Woodpecker	●	●	
50	Steller's Jay	●	●	
53	Brown Pelican	●		
54	California Quail	●	●	●

TRACKING CALIFORNIA'S WILDLIFE PRESERVES

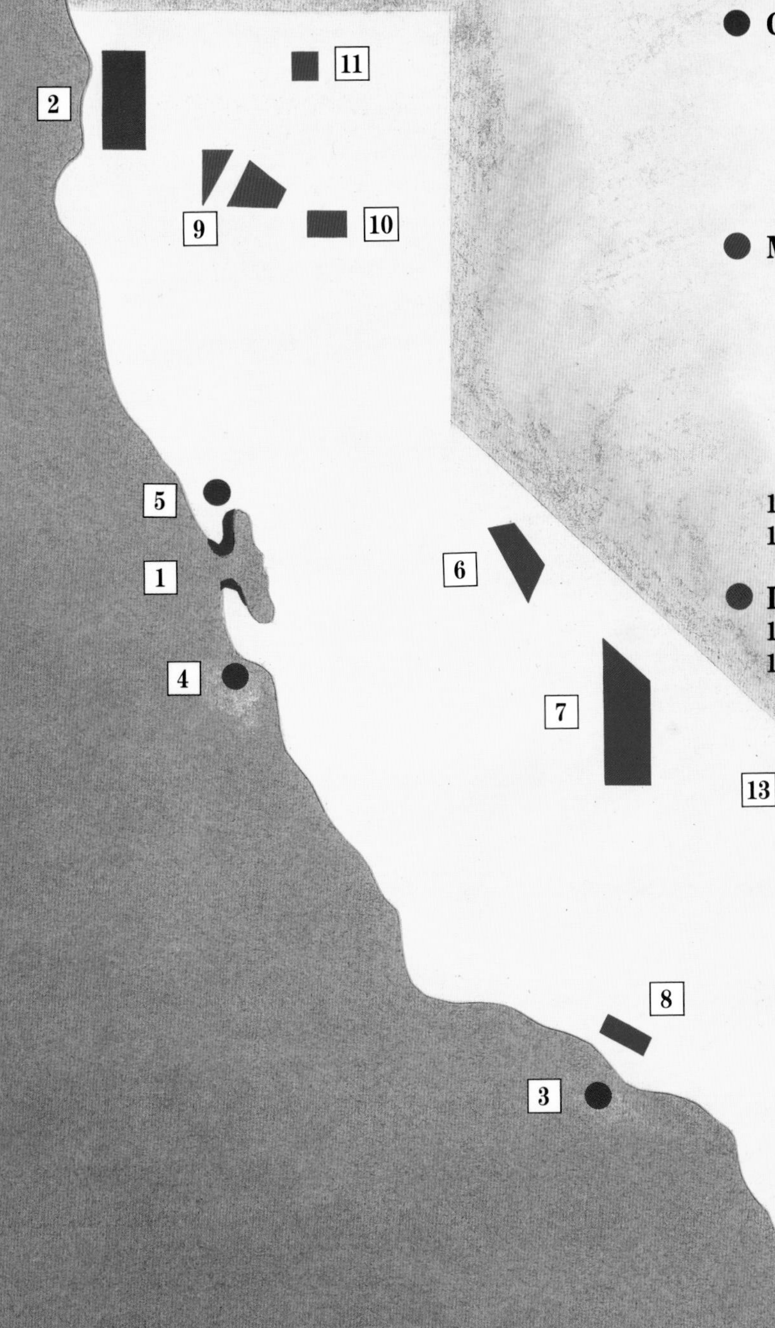

● COASTAL PARKS

1 Golden Gate National Recreation Area
2 Redwood National Park
3 Channel Islands National Park
4 Año Nuevo State Reserve
5 Point Reyes National Seashore

● MOUNTAIN PARKS

6 Yosemite National Park
7 Sequoia and Kings Canyon National Parks
8 Santa Monica Mountains National Recreation Area
9 Whiskeytown-Shasta-Trinity National Recreation Area
10 Lassen Volcanic National Park
11 Lava Beds National Monument

● DESERT PARKS

12 Joshua Tree National Monument
13 Death Valley National Monument

The name black bear can be confusing, since it refers to the animal's species name, not its fur color. Black bears can actually be black, brown, tan, or yellow.

BLACK BEAR

Once the grizzly bear and the black bear roamed the wildlands of California. Today, only the black bear remains. The most likely place to see black bears is in the mountains, where they can live at elevations as high as ten thousand feet. They can also be found along the northern coast, but since they prefer the cooler forested climates, there are very few black bears in southern California and none at all in the desert. Four to five feet long and two to three feet tall when standing on all four feet, black bears generally weigh from two to four hundred pounds, but they can weigh as much as six hundred.

Bears are classified by zoologists as carnivores—animals that eat meat. Black bears, however, are mainly vegetarians, although they eat almost anything, from plants and berries to small animals, like chipmunks and squirrels. This type of eater—one who eats both animals and vegetables—is called omnivorous. The black bear mates every other year, usually in June or July. Seven to nine months later, the female bear, or sow, gives birth to one to four cubs weighing only eight to ten ounces each. Approximately nine inches long at birth, the cubs are blind and have no hair or teeth. Cubs are cared for by their mother for one and a half years.

Black bears are skillful tree climbers and quick runners, able to reach speeds of twenty-five miles per hour. The black bear's only enemy is humans, so look for the bears and their tracks, but don't try to feed or approach them. If you encounter a bear, the best thing to do is to slowly back away and give the bear plenty of space. If you're hiking through the backcountry, sing or talk out loud. This way you will not startle an unsuspecting bear.

MULE DEER

The mule deer can be found in all regions of California: in the mountains, along the coast, and even in the desert. They are often seen at the edge of the forest, where they can hide themselves in leaves and tall grasses. They can also be seen in open meadows, around campgrounds, and at the edge of the road. Their diet consists mainly of leaves and twigs, but they also like to eat wild mushrooms and acorns when they can find them. Mule deer are three to four feet tall and can weigh as much as two hundred pounds.

The male deer, or buck, can be easily distinguished by his large, forked antlers. These antlers are shed every winter and regrown again in the summer. They are covered with a soft, velvety skin while they are developing. When they are completely grown, the skin hardens. Bucks use their antlers both to protect themselves and to compete with other bucks for mates. The mating season of the mule deer occurs every fall and lasts until December. The female deer, or doe, gives birth to one or two fawns in late May or early June. When it is born, the fawn can't walk very well. It spends much of its time curled up in a blanket of leaves on the forest floor. A fawn is born with white spots that act as a camouflage, concealing the young deer from its enemies as its fur blends in with the forest floor. These spots will disappear after two to three months. The young fawn stays with its mother for about one year.

The main enemy of the deer is the mountain lion, although bobcats and coyotes, and even bears, sometimes kill the deer for food. The deer is very fast. It can reach speeds of thirty-five miles an hour and jump as far as twenty-five feet. This quickness helps protect the deer from its enemies.

The mule deer is named for its big ears, which resemble those of a mule. When its ears are erect and forward, the deer is alert and listening carefully. When its ears are laid back, the deer is frightened and trying to hide.

While active both day and night, the coyote is primarily nocturnal. If you listen carefully at dusk or dawn, you might hear coyotes calling each other with a long, mournful howl.

COYOTE

The sly and crafty coyote is probably the most well-adapted mammal in California. Living happily in the desert, the mountains, and along the coast, the coyote can be found at elevations ranging from sea level to ten thousand feet. A member of the dog family, a full-grown coyote is four feet long and weighs from thirty to fifty pounds. Coyotes vary in size and color depending on where they live, but usually have brownish- to reddish-gray fur, long pointy ears, and a black- or brown-tipped tail. The mountain coyote is larger with darker fur, while the desert coyote is smaller and lighter colored.

The coyote is a scavenger and will gladly eat whatever it can find. In the desert it feeds on snakes, spiders, and rats. In the mountains and along the coast, the coyote feeds on squirrels, rabbits, and mice. Even garbage can satisfy a hungry coyote. Coyotes usually hunt alone out in the open, and help control the population of small rodents. The coyote lives underground in a den, beneath the roots of large trees, or in a hill of dirt. These dens often have long tunnels, with many connecting rooms.

The coyote stays with a single mate for years, sometimes for its entire life. Mating occurs from January to February and six to seven pups are born in April or May. The pups weigh seven to ten ounces each and are raised by both parents until they are six months old. The adult coyote's main enemy in the wild is the mountain lion. A young coyote, however, can easily fall into the hungry mouth of a bobcat, a wolverine, or even an eagle.

KIT FOX

A relative of the coyote, the fox is also a member of the dog family. There are four species of foxes living in California: red, gray, island, and kit, but only the desert kit fox is seen with any regularity. Because the desert climate is very hot and dry, the kit fox is nocturnal, spending most of its day underground in a den, waiting for the cooler nighttime weather to search for food. Kit foxes live in dens that were made by some other animal. The den usually has more than one entrance, or escape, that is small enough to keep predators like the badger and the bobcat out. The kit fox can be either brown or gray. It has long ears, a long, bushy black-tipped tail, and black patches on its muzzle.

The kit fox feeds on nocturnal rodents like kangaroo rats, as well as insects, jack rabbits, and cottontails. The mating and raising of young kit foxes, or kits, is very similar to its cousin, the coyote. Although the babies are born a bit earlier, in February or March, their parents have very similar habits. Like the father coyote, the father kit fox moves out of the family den while the pups are born but continues to bring his family food. Baby kits are raised by both their parents and remain with them until autumn.

The kit fox only lives in the low-lying desert regions of California. If you are traveling through some of California's mountain or coastal areas and you are lucky enough to see a fox, it is probably the larger gray fox. You will be able to tell which fox it is from its size. The gray is twice as big as the kit. Currently on California's threatened species list and the federal endangered species list, the kit fox is in danger of becoming extinct primarily because it has fewer places to live due to human expansion.

The kit fox was named for its small size, like a kitten, and is the smallest of the foxes. It weighs a maximum of six pounds and measures fifteen to twenty inches, including its tail.

The raccoon's main enemy is humans. Every year 1.5 million raccoons are killed for their fur, which trappers sell to make fur coats.

RACCOON

The raccoon is often called a bandit because of the black mask across its eyes. Twenty-four to forty-two inches long, including their six-striped tail, most raccoons weigh between ten and twenty-five pounds, although some northern raccoons have been known to weigh as much as fifty pounds. Raccoons are abundant throughout the mountains and coastal regions of California, living in wooded areas along streams and marshes. Since raccoons like water and forested areas, you won't find them in the desert. You also won't see too many during the day, since they are nocturnal animals.

Raccoons are omnivorous, but prefer crayfish, crabs, frogs, turtles, and nesting birds. Raccoons are very clean animals and often wash their food before eating it. Whether this is because it makes the food easier to swallow or because the raccoon enjoys clean food is still being debated by scientists. Raccoons usually live in hollow trees, but they can also happily find shelter in a fallen log, a skunk's ground burrow, or even a vacant building. Raccoons generally have one primary home where they live and breed, and several other dens which they use as temporary homes while they are searching for food.

Raccoons breed in the winter and after about two months, four to five young raccoons are born. The babies weigh twenty ounces at birth and are cared for entirely by their mother. Baby raccoons grow up quickly in the wild: after three weeks their eyes open and after five weeks they are ready to leave the den with their mother. They usually remain with their mother until spring.

PORCUPINE

The porcupine is the second largest rodent and the only quilled mammal native to the United States. Porcupines are good climbers and spend much of their time in trees. While tree bark is their favorite food, porcupines also eat buds, twigs, and even the prickly pear fruits of desert cacti. Porcupines are nocturnal and prefer wooded areas, but have adapted well to all regions of California. The best places to look for them are at the lower elevations and around campgrounds at dusk or at night.

Porcupines usually live alone, except in the winter when several porcupines will den up together to keep warm. Porcupines mate in the late fall. Not much is known about their mating or courting habits, except that it takes seven months for a single baby to be born. A newborn weighs only one pound, measures ten inches, and is covered with hair and soft quills, which harden within the first hour after birth. The young remain with their mother for about six months.

When threatened, the porcupine will run backward into its attacker, poking hundreds of stinging quills into its attacker's skin. The quills have tiny hooks on the end and when stuck are very difficult (and sometimes impossible) to remove. Many animals die from the quills, except coyotes and bobcats, who are able to eat porcupines—quills and all—usually without injury. Porcupines are often criticized for killing trees by scraping off the bark. Sometimes trees do die from infection because of exposure, but the dead trees are used by other animals as homes. Porcupines seem to be attracted to salty wood, and campers have been known to find porcupines gnawing on their canoe paddles and axe handles.

The porcupine's main defense is the thousands of sharp, pointy quills—which are really stiff, hollow hairs—that cover its body.

Unlike other skunks, the striped skunk cannot climb and therefore makes its den on the ground, under rocks or in abandoned burrows.

STRIPED SKUNK

A member of the weasel family, there are three species of skunk: striped, spotted, and hog-nosed. Only the spotted and the striped are found in the West. The spotted skunk is the smallest of all the skunks but is rarely seen. The striped skunk, however, is found throughout the United States (except in Alaska) and in all regions of California. Although active both day and night, the skunk is primarily a nocturnal animal. The best place to find skunks is in campgrounds and along roadsides at lower elevations.

The skunk is a respected member of the wild because of its unusual defense system. It has two glands near the base of its tail, which emit an unpleasant musky spray. If threatened, it will stand and face its enemy, raising its tail in warning. If the enemy continues to approach, the skunk will release its spray. A skunk can accurately spray from a distance of twenty feet or more, temporarily blinding its enemy. The skunk's enemies include owls, coyotes, bobcats, and dogs. If food is scarce, any of these animals will eat the skunk in spite of its smell.

The striped skunk measures thirteen to eighteen inches, not including its long tail, and generally weighs from three to ten pounds. Skunks are omnivorous. They feed mainly on insects and larvae but also eat fruits, vegetables, and berries. Skunks don't hibernate, but they remain in their dens during the coldest months of winter. It is in these winter dens that skunks breed. After two months, a litter of as many as ten (but usually four to five) babies are born. Weighing little more than an ounce at birth, they are hairless with pink skin. Like other mammals this size, baby skunks mature rapidly and are ready to leave their mother at six months.

CALIFORNIA GROUND SQUIRREL

There are over three hundred kinds of squirrels in the world, making the squirrel one of the largest families of rodents. Ground squirrels are the most common squirrels found in California and the easiest to spot. There are many ground squirrels, but the most common species native to California is the California ground squirrel. Sometimes called Beechey's ground squirrel, the California ground squirrel can grow up to eighteen inches long, more than a third of which is its long, bushy tail. The best place to find it is along the northern coast and in the mountains.

The adult California ground squirrel sleeps twice a year. It hibernates in the winter from October to May, depending on the elevation, and again in the heat of the summer at lower elevations or in hot areas. This summer sleep is called estivation. In the fall, ground squirrels eat heavily, putting on thick layers of fat for the winter months. As soon as they emerge from their holes in the spring, the squirrels mate. One month later, four to eight babies are born. Raised solely by their mother, young ground squirrels mature quickly: at five weeks their eyes open and at eight weeks they are ready to leave their burrow. By the time they are eight months old, they are fully grown.

Ground squirrels live in open, dry areas and feed on berries, nuts, seeds, and insects. Like chipmunks, ground squirrels stuff food in their cheeks and store the food in a burrow. The ground squirrel is diurnal, which is the opposite of nocturnal and means that it is most active in the daytime. Because of their size, California ground squirrels fall prey to many. Their chief enemies include hawks, eagles, snakes, and coyotes.

Although this one is alone, California ground squirrels live together in large colonies where they build intricate burrows with many chambers. Sometimes these burrows help prevent soil erosion.

A member of the squirrel family, chipmunks are the only ground squirrel found in North America that have facial stripes.

There are twenty-one different species of chipmunk in North America and eleven in the western Pacific states. If you see a small animal with a single dark stripe running over its eye surrounded by white stripes, you have identified a chipmunk. Exactly what kind of chipmunk you have identified is much harder to determine, since they all look very much the same.

LODGEPOLE CHIPMUNK

The lodgepole chipmunk is the most common chipmunk in California and can be found in all regions. It adapts well to the high mountain areas as well as the lower desert elevations. At lower elevations, chipmunks are active all year. At the higher elevations, they hibernate during the winter. Chipmunks forage for food on the ground but can climb trees as well as any squirrel. They collect pine nuts and acorns by stuffing them into their cheeks. Then they store the food by burying the nuts in small holes to be saved for winter. A chipmunk doesn't always remember all its hiding places. A forgotten nut can grow into the seedling for a new tree, so without knowing it, chipmunks help to maintain the forest.

Chipmunks make their home in a hole up in a tree, in old rotten logs, or in loose dirt where they can easily dig tunnels. Three to six babies are born each spring and remain with their mother for a short six weeks. The mother will often have two litters in one year, mating again before the end of the summer. Despite their rapid reproduction, the chipmunk population is controlled by two factors: they have a short life span, and, because of their small size, they have many enemies. Among the chipmunk's main predators are foxes, coyotes, hawks, and snakes.

DESERT COTTONTAIL

The cottontail is a mammal and a member of the rabbit family. Rabbits are characterized by long ears, short tails, and long hind legs. The cottontail is one of the most hunted animals in the wild. Many cottontails are killed each year by both man and animal, but they continue to thrive because of their incredible rate of reproduction. Cottontails may have as many as seven litters in one year. Each litter averages three babies. They are born blind and virtually hairless, but within four weeks they are able to leave their mother's nest and can have families of their own. The cottontails' mating habits are quite distinctive: one leaps high in the air while the other darts underneath it.

Cottontails are seldom found in the forest. They prefer the edges of meadows and brushlands where they live under the cover of a bush or cactus rather than in a burrow. The desert cottontail is common in all the desert regions of California and is active both day and night. If you find yourself in one of the mountain or coastal parks, you are more likely to see its cousin, the brush rabbit.

Primarily herbivorous, cottontails feed on grass and herbs in the summer, and tree bark and twigs in the winter. The cottontail's lifespan is very short, less than a year, because it is preyed upon so heavily by bobcats, coyotes, foxes, snakes, owls, and hawks. When frightened by a predator, this rabbit will freeze in its tracks and then raise its tail to alert other cottontails. When raised, the white underside of the tail stands out to give warning to all the cottontails to run for cover. Once safely in the brush, the cottontail lowers its tail and becomes hidden.

The desert cottontail can be easily identified by its big ears and fluffy white tail—which looks like a ball of cotton—from which it got its name.

Fully protected by law, the desert tortoise is on the threatened species list primarily because of land development, off-road vehicles (like motorcycles, dirtbikes, and jeeps), and illegal collecting.

DESERT TORTOISE

The desert tortoise is the only species of tortoise native to California. While an adult tortoise may grow to be fifteen inches long, most are less than eight inches long and all begin as two-inch hatchlings. Young tortoises have soft, leathery shells which develop into strong armor after approximately five years. When the tortoise is in danger, it retreats inside its shell. The adult's shell is so thick that no predator, no matter how sharp its teeth or claws, can penetrate it. But many tortoises never live to be five years old because their soft, immature shells make them easy targets for predators.

The desert tortoise is a member of the reptile family. All reptiles are ectothermic, or cold-blooded, which means they can't maintain a constant body temperature. To protect itself from extreme changes in temperature, the tortoise hibernates during the winter when temperatures are too cold and in the summer it avoids the midday heat by retreating underground. But the tortoise's most unique adaption to the desert climate is its ability to store water. The desert tortoise has its own reservoir beneath its shell. This reservoir is so big it can hold enough water to last an entire season. When water is available, the tortoise will drink and drink, like a camel, storing the water in its reservoir to be saved for the desert's long dry spells.

The desert tortoise is herbivorous, feeding solely on plants like herbs, grass, and cacti. The tortoise hibernates from October to March in a burrow three feet below the ground. In June, the female tortoise lays between two and six eggs, each about the size of a golf ball. She hides them at the entrance to her burrow in a shallow hole, by covering them with sand.

SIDEWINDER

The sidewinder is a nocturnal reptile and a member of the rattlesnake family. Rattlesnakes are named for a series of loosely interlocking horny segments at the end of their tails. When shaken, these segments make a rattling sound to warn approaching predators of the snake's presence. Snakes shed their skin several times a year by loosening the skin around their mouth and head, and then rubbing their nose on a rough surface. The snake then crawls out of the old skin, turning it inside out. This process is called molting. Rattlesnakes molt about two or three times a year, and less frequently as they grow older.

Seventeen to thirty-three inches in length, the sidewinder is often called the horned rattler because of its pointed horn-like eyes. The sidewinder blends into its background with lightly patterned blotches running down its back and a dark stripe across its eyes. It lives in desert flats, sand dunes, and rocky hillsides where it can find shelter beneath rocks. Under these rocks, five to eighteen babies are born each fall. Some baby reptiles, like the sidewinder, are born alive, rather than in a shell. The sidewinder is often found near rodent burrows where it hunts pocket mice, kangaroo rats, and lizards, or, in open terrain where it can move along in its sideways S-pattern more freely. Because of this distinct movement, the sidewinder is easy to track by looking for the S-shaped curves it leaves behind in the sand.

The sidewinder is a poisonous snake carrying a dangerous venom in its fangs. If threatened, the snake bites its enemy to release the poison. Most people believe that all snakes are poisonous. While this is true of the rattlesnake family, it is not true of all snakes.

Scientists believe that snakes developed from lizards over one million years ago. Over time, snakes lost their feet and now they often coil their flexible bodies into a tight circle.

Even though the side-blotched lizard is the most abundant lizard found in California's deserts, they rarely live more than two years.

SIDE-BLOTCHED LIZARD

The side-blotched lizard is the most common reptile of the western desert, where it is found in abundance. One to three inches long, this tiny lizard has brown scaly skin and clawed toes. It can be recognized by a bluish-black blotch on each side of its chest, behind its front legs. Although the side-blotched lizard is diurnal, it rests in the afternoon during the desert's hottest hours. It can be seen on cooler days and in the morning and early evening.

Lizards are cold-blooded reptiles and are closely related to snakes. Cold-blooded means that they can't keep their bodies much warmer or cooler than the temperature of their surroundings. To compensate, the lizard warms itself in the hot sun or on a warm rock and when it gets too hot, it cools its body in the shade. Lizards have long, brittle tails which break quite easily. Sometimes when an enemy seizes the lizard, the lizard's tail breaks off, allowing the lizard to crawl to safety. Meanwhile, the tail keeps moving as though it were alive, fooling the enemy and giving the lizard time to escape. In time, the lizard simply grows a new tail.

The side-blotched lizard is active all year long and can be seen in sandy, rocky areas where it can hide in grass or shrubs. Living close to the ground, this lizard likes to eat insects, scorpions, spiders, and ticks. Sometimes you can see this lizard playfully leaping into the air to catch flying insects. The female usually lays from two to seven batches, or clutches, of eggs each year from March to August. Each clutch will contain from one to eight eggs.

GRAY WHALE

Whales are marine (or aquatic) mammals, which means that they spend their whole life in the ocean. Whales have three distinguishing features: flukes, a blowhole, and blubber. The horizontal extensions on the end of the whale's tail are called flukes. The whale's swimming power comes from the muscles located in its back which move the flukes up and down. The whale's nostril opening, located on the top of its head, is called the blowhole. The blowhole allows the whale to breathe. Blubber is the thick layer of fat beneath their skin, which insulates the whale against heat loss and extreme cold waters. There are two types of whales: toothed and baleen. Toothed whales have jaws with one or more pairs of teeth. Baleen whales, like the gray whale, are toothless with hundreds of thin plates, called baleen, hanging from the jaw. The baleen is used to strain food. The gray whale feeds mainly on plankton and tiny invertebrates.

Living only in the North Pacific Ocean, the gray whale averages in length from thirty-five to fifty feet and weighs twenty-five to thirty-five tons. Its migration, thirteen thousand miles roundtrip, is the longest migration of any mammal. Gray whales migrate south from the Arctic in the early fall to the warm lagoons of Baja, California to spend the winter and to give birth to their young. Gray whales usually give birth only once in two years. After a period of twelve months, the female, or cow, gives birth in protected lagoons to a single calf fourteen to seventeen feet long and weighing up to fifteen hundred pounds.

The gray whale can be seen all along California's coast from December to January and again from March to May. Viewing is best on the whales' trip north from March to May, when cows and calves often come in closer to the coast.

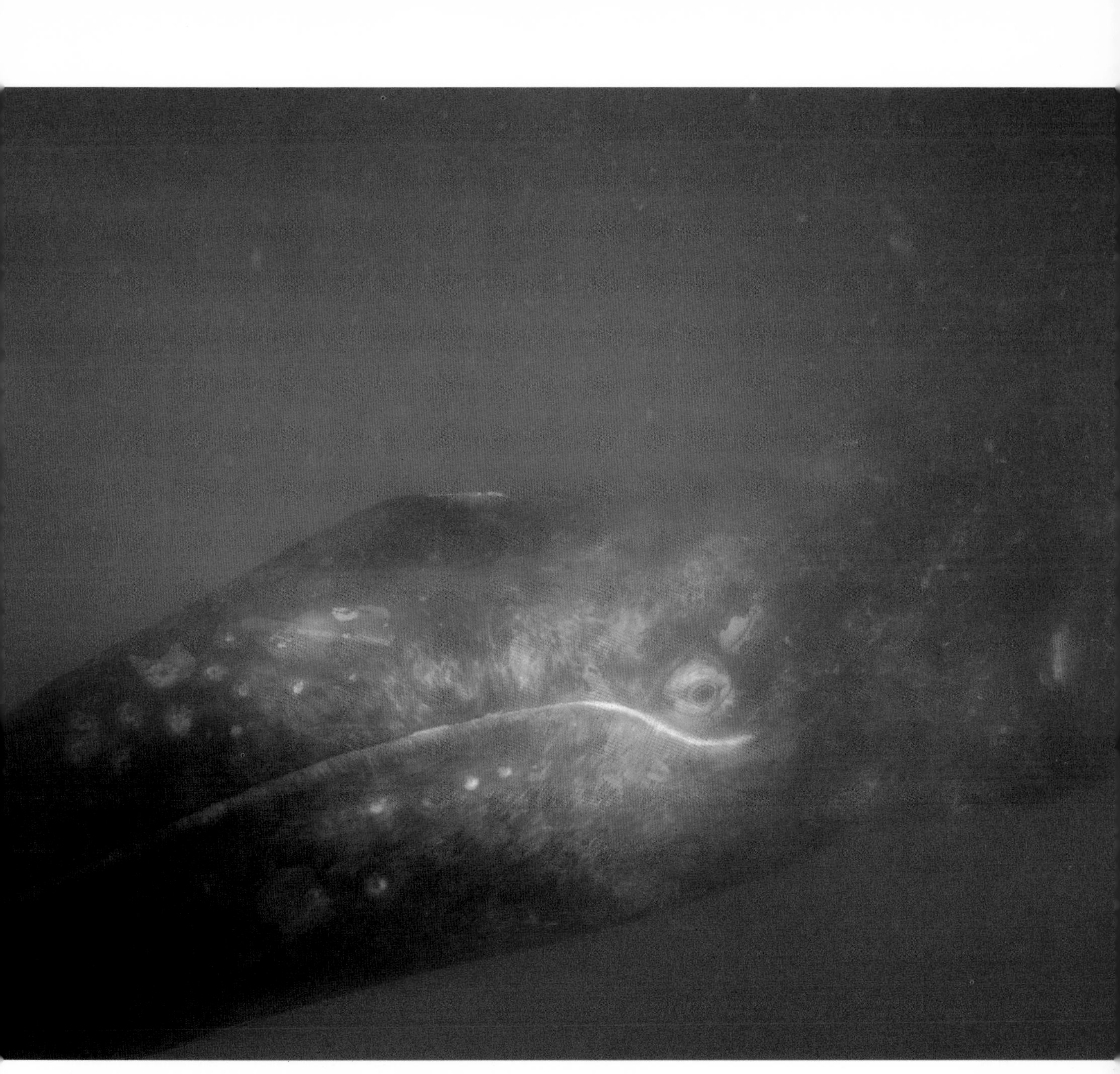

Since 1946 the gray whale has been under the complete protection of federal laws and although it was once almost extinct, the gray whale numbers close to twenty thousand today.

Once hunted to near extinction, the northern elephant seal is now fully protected by law. On the rise today, there are believed to be over two thousand, five hundred at Año Nuevo State Reserve alone, their favorite breeding spot.

The northern elephant seal is the largest and most powerful member of the pinniped family, which consists of seals, sea lions, and walrus. Pinnipeds are aquatic mammals whose four limbs have been modified into flippers. Pinnipeds have a thick layer of fat under their skin, which sometimes amounts to one third of their total body weight. This blubber insulates the elephant seal from the cold Pacific waters, as well as allowing the seal to float. The elephant seal's diet consists mainly of squid, small sharks, and fish.

The massive male, or bull, elephant seal can grow to be seventeen feet long and weigh five thousand pounds, while the female is about one third the size. The bull can be distinguished by its enlarged, elephant-like nose, which may grow to be a foot long. Elephant seals breed from December to February, fasting for the entire season. A single pup is born about a week after the female arrives at the breeding ground, or rookery, although it has been growing inside its mother for eight to nine months. She takes care of the pup for a month, abandoning it only to mate again before it is time to leave the rookery. Four feet long, weighing eighty to one hundred pounds at birth, the pup grows quickly. After just eleven days the pup may double its weight and after a month, it may triple its size.

Northern elephant seals can be seen all along the coast from Baja north to Point Reyes. Most of the time, elephant seals are far out at sea and so are difficult to find. The two exceptions are in the winter during their breeding season, and in spring and early summer when they come ashore to molt. This is the best time to look for the elephant seal at Año Nuevo State Reserve.

CALIFORNIA SEA LION

The barking of California sea lions is a familiar sound all along California's rocky coast. A very swift swimmer, the California sea lion is capable of reaching speeds of up to twenty-five miles per hour. Often you will see it floating along the water's surface with one flipper raised. You may think the sea lion is waving to you, but it is actually regulating its body temperature by taking in or releasing heat through its flipper. The sea lion can dive as deep as four hundred feet, remaining under water for up to twenty minutes in search of its favorite foods: mollusks, squid, octopi, herring, and crustaceans.

California sea lions breed from June to July in rookeries found on southern California's Channel Islands and islands off of Baja, California. Bulls become very aggressive and territorial during mating season, each controlling a harem numbering as many as fifteen females, or cows. The cows remain at the rookery throughout the year, while the bulls roam the entire coast. About a year later, one pup is born weighing only twelve pounds and measuring just two and a half feet. While the pup is young, it is a prime target for the sea lion's main enemies: killer whales and great white sharks. The adult's most feared enemy, however, is the commercial fisherman's net. Sea lions often become entangled in these nets and die before they can be released.

Distinguished by its dark brown fur, the California sea lion averages six feet, two hundred forty pounds for females, and eight feet, seven hundred and fifteen pounds for males. Today there are a total of one hundred and fifty thousand California sea lions along the western coast of North America. Half of these are found off of California's shores.

Rarely found more than ten miles offshore, most of the time California sea lions can be seen lazily sunning themselves on rocks, secluded beaches, and on top of buoys.

The sea otter's large flipper hind feet are used to propel the otter through the water, while its small hand-like forepaws are used for catching food.

SEA OTTER

The largest member of the weasel family, sea otters average five to six feet in length and can weigh up to one hundred pounds. The sea otter eats as much as one fifth of its total body weight each day, feeding on invertebrates like crab, abalones, snails, and sea urchin. Lying on its back, the otter will sandwich its food between two rocks and clap the rocks together until the shell breaks. Since sea otters seem to be constantly eating, if you listen carefully you can usually hear this clacking sound when there are otters around.

Otters are very clean animals and spend much of their time grooming their coats. Keeping its fur clean is essential to the sea otter's survival. Sea otters lack the thick layer of blubber found in many other marine mammals, so their fine, dense fur is all they have to insulate themselves from the cold Pacific waters. To sleep, the sea otter wraps sea kelp around its middle to prevent its body from drifting. Mating takes place in the water, usually in the fall. When the mother is ready, she heads for the safety of the kelp beds, where she gives birth to a single pup weighing four pounds. Because the sea otter must give birth and take care of its young entirely in the water, having more than one is too difficult, though twins do occur on rare occasion. Baby sea otters spend most of their time lying on their mother's chest, staying clear of enemy sharks and killer whales.

The California sea otter population is restricted to the region from San Luis Obispo County north to San Mateo County. In 1989 there were approximately two thousand sea otters in these areas, most of which live off the coast of Monterey and Point Lobos. The sea otter has been federally protected since 1910, but even today it remains on the threatened species list.

GOLDEN EAGLE

Eagles are the second largest raptor in North America, after the California condor. The word raptor is used to describe birds of prey that have three distinct features: hooked upper beaks; feet with sharp claws, called talons; and excellent vision. Raptors include eagles, hawks, and owls. While our national symbol, the bald eagle, is the largest eagle at forty inches long, the golden eagle is close behind at thirty-seven inches long with a wingspan of over seven feet.

The golden eagle hunts for food by day, flying low to the ground in search of small rodents and rabbits. Golden eagles kill their prey with their strong grip and sharp talons, which are approximately nine inches long. As a member of the hawk family, the eagle is able to consume all the parts of its prey, including bones and fur. Golden eagles build huge stick nests, called aeries, on steep cliff ledges or in tall trees. The eagles reuse the same nests year after year, always adding new materials. While a new nest is usually five to six feet, an old nest may reach ten feet across and fifteen feet deep, and weigh a ton or more. The female usually lays her eggs in March and five to six weeks later, they hatch. The young eagle, called an eaglet, is born with its eyes open and is covered with fuzzy down. Real feathers begin to grow when the eaglet is three weeks old. Cared for by both parents, the young eaglet leaves home after ten to twelve weeks.

Although the golden eagle can be found in all regions of California, it is currently on the protected species list, making it a rare find. The best place to look for it is in the desert and mountain regions where it breeds in the summer.

The golden eagle must turn its entire head to see from left to right, as its eyes are basically immobile within their sockets. But these excellent radar eyes are capable of spotting prey as far as two miles away.

Although red-tailed hawks may seem to be searching for prey as they glide through the air, they often locate their target from high, exposed perches before taking flight.

RED-TAILED HAWK

The red-tailed hawk is one of the largest and most common hawks in North America. In California, it can be seen soaring all year throughout different regions: through canyons; above mountain meadows; across the desert; along rivers and the coast. The red-tailed hawk is recognized by the broad reddish tail that gives the bird its name. A typical adult has a brown head, a light-colored chest, and a dark-streaked band of feathers on the belly. Red-tailed hawks prey on all kinds of small birds, as well as ground squirrels, mice, snakes, and lizards. As a member of the raptor group, hawks use a direct dive to stun unsuspecting prey and will sometimes eat their meal in mid-air. The hawk's stomach is very acidic, allowing it to devour entire birds—feathers, fur, bones, and all! Later, the hawk will cough up a pellet, containing the parts of the prey it can't use.

There are two main types of hawks: accipiters and buteos. The red-tailed hawk is a buteo, characterized by its long, blunt wings and short tail, which spread out like a fan in flight. Accipiters, on the other hand, are medium-sized hawks with short, rounded wings and a much longer tail. Male and female red-tailed hawks have the same coloration, but the females are usually larger. It takes a young red-tailed hawk two years to reach adult plumage.

Sometimes mating for life, the red-tailed hawk builds its nest between the forked limbs of tall trees or in a cliff face. This nest will be reused year after year, unless a great horned owl (who never builds its own nest) takes over. The female hawk usually lays one to three eggs which hatch after thirty days. Young red-tailed hawks remain in the nest for one to two months.

GREAT HORNED OWL

The great horned owl is the largest and most widely distributed owl in North America. Owls are distinguished by their large eyes, short, thick bodies, strong hooked beaks, and powerful feet with sharp claws. The great horned owl is almost two feet long with a white throat, grayish-brown plumage, and large ear tufts that look like horns.

Primarily a nocturnal bird of prey, owls are capable of swiveling their heads almost all the way around, easily scanning their surroundings for prey. Although cottontails make up approximately half of the great horned owl's diet, it easily snatches birds, snakes, and rodents, and will even take animals as large as porcupines and skunks. Because they are active only at night, and because they are well hidden in the trees, owls are very difficult to spot. The best way to find one is not to look up in the trees but to search the ground beneath the trees for their white droppings and pellets.

The great horned owl prefers to live in open, forested mountain regions, but can also be seen in desert, plain, canyon, and scrub areas. Owls are noisiest in January and February, during their breeding season. Their call consists of four to seven low, unevenly spaced hoots that can often be heard at dusk or dawn. Owls never build their own nests but instead occupy nests abandoned by ravens or hawks. The female lays two to three eggs, which hatch after four weeks. Young owls mature slowly, remaining in the nest for ten weeks before taking their first flight. Because the owl is the top predator in its food chain, they have few enemies except humans.

The great horned owl is distinguished by the large tufted ears on the top of its head. These tufts have nothing to do with the owl's excellent hearing, however; they are really for camouflage.

Distinguished by its striking black plumage and shaggy feathers, the common raven has strong feet and toes for catching prey and tearing flesh, and a strong curved beak.

COMMON RAVEN

Averaging twenty-two to twenty-seven inches in length, with a wingspan of four feet or more, the common raven is the largest member of the crow family. The all-black raven is often mistaken for a crow, but is nearly twice the size. Its loud, deep voice can be heard throughout California where it lives a very social lifestyle. The common raven lives in pairs or small groups, but can be seen roosting in groups of up to a hundred. The raven is common in the most rugged desert habitats in California, as well as along the coast and in the mountains.

The raven is omnivorous, feeding on anything from large insects, small birds and mammals, to fruit. Like other members of the crow family, the raven will bury excess food in the ground in case food becomes scarce, though it rarely returns to retrieve its cache. The raven is a scavenger and its favorite feast includes garbage or carrion (carcasses of dead animals). The raven is a playful bird, often showing off for a mate with aerial acrobatics. The raven soars, tumbles, and rolls through the air as it tries to please a potential mate. Gathering its courage, it will sometimes challenge the mighty eagle or a hawk to an aerial fight.

The common raven mates in the air and then nests in rocky cliffs or in tall trees. The female lays three to six spotted eggs in February or March, which hatch after an eighteen-day incubation period. The raven is a tidy bird; after the babies, called nestlings, hatch, the female swallows the eggshells to clean out the nest. Cared for by both parents, the young raven will stay in its mother's nest for five to six weeks.

ROADRUNNER

The roadrunner is a member of the cuckoo family, specifically of the ground cuckoo species. Cuckoos are known for placing their eggs in the nests of other birds, tricking the unsuspecting bird into raising the cuckoos' young. In some cuckoo species, like the roadrunner, the parents actually raise their own young. The roadrunner is a swift, ground-dwelling bird associated with the desert regions of the West, but also occasionally found in chaparral, grasslands, and the open woodland areas of mountain parks.

The roadrunner's name comes from the bird's habit of racing down roads in front of moving vehicles and then darting to safety in the brush. While the roadrunner can fly, it is most comfortable on the ground where it can reach speeds as fast as fifteen miles per hour, though only for short distances. Two feet in length, half of which is tail, the roadrunner has long sturdy legs and a pointed bill. Distinguished by a brown upper body with black streaks and white spots, its neck is white or pale brown, and it has a white belly. When excited, the roadrunner will raise its crest revealing a triangle of white skin behind the eye which first turns blue and then bright red.

The roadrunner builds its nest out of twigs in low trees or cacti. The female lays two to six eggs which hatch after eighteen days. While the eggs are developing, the male, rather than the female, incubates them. One to three weeks after birth, the young roadrunner can catch its own food and is ready to run off on its own.

The roadrunner's main food is grasshoppers, but it also enjoys insects, mice, lizards, and snakes. After the roadrunner catches its prey, it beats the animal against a rock until it dies and then swallows the food whole.

The acorn woodpecker has strong feet with two toes facing forward and two facing back, while most other birds have three toes forward and one back. This unique characteristic helps to balance the woodpecker against tree trunks.

ACORN WOODPECKER

The acorn woodpecker is one of the more familiar Sierran woodpeckers. Like most other woodpeckers, it is distinguished by a bright red crown and light-colored eyes. As its name suggests, the acorn woodpecker's favorite food is acorns, although like other woodpeckers, it also eats insects. The woodpecker uses its long chisel-like bill to drill holes in tree trunks, telephone poles, and even houses for storing the acorn nuts it gathers. It has strong head muscles which act as cushions to protect the skull from the constant hammering and a long, sticky tongue to pull insects from the hole. The acorn woodpecker has strong feet and sharp claws which enable it to climb up and down tree trunks, while its stiff tail feathers brace the bird against the trunk.

This woodpecker lives in a very tight social family, which is unique among birds. The acorn woodpecker lives in what is called a cooperative breeding group. In this group, three or more adults defend the nest as helpers, while one pair actually breeds. The acorn woodpecker drills a hole in a tree approximately one foot deep and lays two to eight eggs in this nest. The chicks hatch two weeks later and are cared for by both parents and other members of their group. About a year later, the young woodpecker is ready to go off on its own.

Because of its love of acorns, it is not surprising that the acorn woodpecker prefers to live in the oak trees which grow the seeds. The acorn woodpecker can be found in both mountain and coastal regions but prefers the woodlands and foothills of the forest.

STELLER'S JAY

The Steller's jay is a medium-sized jay and a member of the crow family. The Steller's jay has white lines between its eyes, as well as richly colored blue wings and tail. It is often mistaken for its relatives, the blue jay or the scrub jay, both of which are paler in color and lack the Steller's crest. One of the best known birds in the Sierra, this crested jay can also be seen along the coast or anywhere with well-shaded forests and piney woodlands.

The Steller's jay was named after the German naturalist Georg Wilhelm Steller, who discovered the bird in 1741 on a Russian expedition to Alaska. The jay is omnivorous, feeding on anything from seeds, insects, and fruit, to small animals and other birds' eggs. In the winter, the jay's diet consists almost solely of seeds like acorns and pine nuts. Not much is known of the Steller's jay's mating habits, but it is known to breed in April and May. The jay builds a nest lined with tree roots and made out of sticks, where it lays five to seven eggs. The eggs hatch after sixteen days and the young are taken care of for approximately three weeks.

The Steller's jay is a noisy mimic and can often be heard imitating other birds, like the red-tailed hawk. This aggressive jay is also known as a robber jay because it steals eggs from other birds' nests, as well as digging into an acorn woodpecker's cache of acorns. Steller's jays are even so bold as to quickly take crumbs and other handouts from generous campers. But don't expect this bird to wait for an invitation. If given half a chance it will fly right down into your picnic and steal the food off your plate.

The Steller's jay is a common bird found in piney woods throughout California. The female and male look alike and are easily identified by a dark bluish-black crest on the top of their head.

The friendly brown pelican is rarely territorial or aggressive and will gladly share its rock or feeding ground with other birds. The smallest of its species, the brown pelican is four feet long with a wingspan of seven feet.

BROWN PELICAN

The pelican is easily recognized by the flexible pouch on the underside of its bill, where it stores fish it has caught. In addition to a long, straight bill, pelicans have webbed feet which make them strong swimmers. The adult has a white head and dark grayish-brown body, while a young pelican is all dark with a white belly.

The brown pelican is the most common North American pelican and lives only along the coast. A skilled flier, it will glide along until it sees a fish near the surface of the water. Then it will dive head first, straight into the water to catch the fish. The California brown pelican eats mackerel, sardines, anchovies, and herring. Almost always seen in flocks, the brown pelican nests in colonies in the Channel Islands off the coast of southern California. Upon reaching its nesting grounds in May and June, each female lays two to three eggs that hatch after four weeks. The babies are cared for by both parents, eating fish from their pouches for six weeks. The young pelican matures slowly and is two months old before its powerful feathers have developed enough to enable the bird to fly.

The California brown pelican is on the endangered species list. It has been threatened by pollution, primarily from pesticides and oil spills. These toxins get into the waters, contaminating the food of the pelican and other California animals. When a pelican eats the contaminated food, it may die. Toxins can also cause the female's eggs to have thin, fragile shells. This results in fewer babies hatching and thus a decrease in the population.

CALIFORNIA QUAIL

There are over a hundred species of quail in the world, seven of which can be found in the United States. The three common western species are California, Gambel's, and mountain. The California quail was originally found only in California, which is how it got its name. Today, however, its territory has expanded throughout the Pacific states. The California quail is distinguished by a curved, protruding topknot on its head and a jet-black throat. The quail prefers the oak and brushy slopes and valleys of the coast, but can be seen in backyard gardens, vineyards, city parks, and the desert.

The quail is a gregarious bird and lives in large groups, called coveys. In the fall, five to six families will flock together to endure the cold winter. Mating occurs from early April to late May, and the cock's (male's) call can be heard throughout the breeding area. The cock displays himself to the hen, bowing and dancing around her, as he chatters mating sounds. The hen lays twelve to sixteen cream-colored spotted eggs in a hidden nest lined with grass. The chicks are lively immediately after birth, but cannot fly for a week to ten days. They are striped with downy feathers, and have a miniature topknot on their head to match their parents'. Cared for by both parents, the young quail is independent after just four weeks.

The California quail feeds on seeds, grain, insects, and other small invertebrates. Reluctant to fly, the quail remains close to the ground and avoids tall vegetation where it may not see an approaching enemy. The quail prefers to stay out in the open, keeping alert for the hungry hawks and ravens that hunt it.

A familiar sight throughout the state, the California quail was declared California's state bird in 1931.

GLOSSARY

accipiter: a bird-eating forest hawk with short wings and a long tail.

aquatic: a type of animal that grows, lives, or spends most of its time in the water.

baleen: thin plates hanging from the jaw of a whale. Baleen whales have two rows of baleen instead of teeth.

burrow: a hole in the ground made by an animal for shelter and habitation.

buteo: a soaring hawk with long, rounded wings and a short tail.

cache: a hiding place especially for storing food or provisions.

camouflage: color and patterns that help an animal or plant blend into its surroundings.

carnivore: an animal whose diet consists mainly of meat.

crustacean: aquatic animals that have an external skeleton, modified legs, and two pairs of antennae. Includes lobsters, shrimps and crabs.

diurnal: an animal that is active in the daytime.

ecology: a branch of science concerned with the relationship between organisms and their environment.

ectothermic: an animal having a body temperature that is not internally regulated but affected by its environment; cold-blooded.

endangered species: a group of animals threatened with extinction.

estivation: the summer resting period of hibernation.

habitat: the place where a plant or animal lives and grows.

herbivore: an animal whose diet consists mainly of plants.

hibernate: a period of rest or inactivity, usually in winter.

invertebrate: an animal without a spinal column or backbone.

mammal: a class of animals covered with hair that feed milk to their young. Hair can be fur, wool, quills, and even certain horns.

marine mammal: an aquatic animal that lives in salt water.

migrate: to move from one place to another for food or to breed.

mollusk: a group of invertebrate animals with a soft body enclosed in a shell. Includes snails, clams, and mussels.

molt: to shed an outer layer of skin, hair, feathers, shell, or horns.

nocturnal: an animal that is active at night.

omnivore: an animal that feeds on both plants and animals.

predator: an animal that catches and devours another animal.

protected species: a group of animals protected by state or federal law because they are either endangered or threatened.

raptor: a bird of prey with a hooked beak, sharp talons, and excellent vision. Includes owls, hawks, and eagles.

reptile: an ectothermic animal with scales that moves on its belly or on short, small legs. Includes lizards, snakes, and turtles.

species: a biological group of animals or plants that breed with one another and share the same general physical characteristics.

threatened species: a group of animals whose numbers are decreasing, bringing the group close to endangerment.

venom: a poison transmitted to prey by biting or stinging.

zoology: the study of animals. A zoologist is one who studies zoology.